Incarnation
Leader Guide

INCARNATION
REDISCOVERING THE SIGNIFICANCE OF CHRISTMAS

Incarnation: Rediscovering the Significance of Christmas
978-1-7910-0554-2 *Hardcover with jacket*
978-1-7910-0555-9 *eBook*
978-1-7910-0556-6 *Large Print*

Incarnation: DVD
978-1-7910-0559-7

Incarnation: Youth Study Book
978-1-7910-0564-1
978-1-7910-0565-8 eBook

Incarnation: Leader Guide
978-1-7910-0557-3
978-1-7910-0558-0 eBook

**Incarnation:
Children's Leader Guide**
978-1-7910-0553-5

Also by Adam Hamilton

24 Hours That Changed the World

Christianity and World Religions

Christianity's Family Tree

Confronting the Controversies

Creed

Enough

Faithful

Final Words from the Cross

Forgiveness

Half Truths

John

Leading Beyond the Walls

Love to Stay

Making Sense of the Bible

Moses

Not a Silent Night

Revival

*Seeing Gray in a World
of Black and White*

Selling Swimsuits in the Arctic

Simon Peter

Speaking Well

The Call

The Journey

The Walk

The Way

Unafraid

Unleashing the Word

When Christians Get It Wrong

Why?

For more information, visit www.AdamHamilton.com.

ADAM HAMILTON

Author of *The Journey*, *Not a Silent Night*, and *Faithful*

INCARNATION

REDISCOVERING THE SIGNIFICANCE OF CHRISTMAS

Leader Guide
by Mike Poteet

Abingdon Press/Nashville

Incarnation:
Rediscovering the Significance of Christmas
Leader Guide

978-1-7910-0557-3

20 21 22 23 24 25 26 27 28 29—10 9 8 7 6 5 4 3 2 1
MANUFACTURED IN THE UNITED STATES OF AMERICA

CONTENTS

INTRODUCTION

In *Incarnation*, the Reverend Adam Hamilton explores seven titles for Jesus used in the New Testament stories of Jesus's birth.

Christians hear and use most of these titles for Jesus throughout the year. But by considering these names and images specifically in the context of Jesus's Nativity, Hamilton demonstrates the extent to which "the Christmas story," familiar both to believers and to the culture at large, truly is the Gospel story. These titles help us move beyond simplified, sentimental understandings of the story to recognize, celebrate, and act upon its deep truths about who Jesus is and what his coming means.

This Leader Guide is designed to help you guide your small group through a four-session study of *Incarnation*. It offers opportunities to review and reflect on the main points and themes of Hamilton's book, and you will gain the most from it if group members have read or are reading *Incarnation*. The sessions contain quotes from Hamilton's book as discussion prompts and are organized around key scripture passages from the book.

Each session corresponds to one chapter from *Incarnation*, although the fourth session also includes material from the book's Epilogue:

- **Session 1: Presidents and Kings:** In this session, participants will explore what Jesus's first followers meant when they called him *King* and *Messiah*, and how calling Jesus *King* can help us grow in faith and obedience today.

- **Session 2: The Savior and Our Need for Saving:** In this session, participants will reflect on the literal meaning of Jesus's name and consider how Jesus has saved us, is saving us, and will save us.

- **Session 3: Emmanuel in the Midst of a Pandemic:** In this session, participants will explore how the message of "Emmanuel" was one of hope in both the Old and New Testaments, and how it can still be a message of hope in times of sadness, doubt, and fear today.

- **Session 4: Light of the World, Word of God, and Lord:** In this session, participants will discover how Christmas is both a celebration of God's response to darkness and God's call for us to respond as well.

Each session in this Leader's Guide contains the following parts:

- **Session Objectives:** Keep these in mind, along with your group's interests and personalities, as you choose from the questions and activities provided to plan your session.

- **Biblical Foundations:** Key Old and New Testament texts, in the New Revised Standard Version, on which the material in each session is based.

- **Sample Session Plan:** Each session contains needed preparatory steps to take, suggested opening icebreakers and activities, questions for discussing *Incarnation* and the companion DVD, closing activities, and optional extensions, as well as an opening and a closing prayer. You likely won't be able to use all the material provided, so choose the questions and activities you think fit your group best.

To help your group study of *Incarnation* succeed, you will want to do the following:

- Promote your study within and beyond your congregation well in advance, especially if you will be using it during what tends to be the busy Advent season.
- Secure a comfortable and inviting meeting space, physically accessible to all participants. Ideally, participants will be seated in a circle so everyone can see one another. Movable chairs will help facilitate the formation of pairs or small groups, suggested in several sessions. (See the notes on pages 10–11 on virtual meetings.)
- Have an easel with large sheets of paper or a markerboard and erasable markers to write group responses and make lists.

- If you plan to use multimedia technology, as suggested in some sessions, test your equipment before each session to be sure it works.
- Bring a supply of Bibles for participants who forget or do not have their own. Include a variety of translations.
- Begin and end on time to respect participants' schedules and the gift of their presence and involvement.
- Create a climate of openness, encouraging group members to participate freely while respecting opinions and points of view different from their own. Be aware of signs of discomfort from those who remain silent; encourage their participation, but also assure all participants their verbal participation is not mandatory. Give everyone the chance to talk, but keep conversations moving!

A Note on Virtual Meetings

With some creativity and patience on everyone's part, you can adapt these sessions for virtual, online use using such platforms as Zoom. Should you want or need to meet virtually:

- Communicate all online meeting details (websites, passwords, beginning time, and so forth) to participants well in advance of each session. Create and use an email distribution list, putting your study's name in the subject line so recipients can spot and refer to the email easily. If possible, post contact information for your study (but

not each session's log-on information) on your
congregation's website.

- If using video in your virtual meeting, be sure
  you, as the leader, are sitting in a well-lit and quiet
  place in front of a background with few or no
  distractions. Encourage group participants to do
  likewise.

- Agree with your members on a group protocol for
  recognizing who "has the floor." For example, will
  participants agree to wait until no one is speaking
  to answer a question? Will they need to "raise their
  hand" (physically or digitally) before speaking?
  Establishing and sticking with some basic ground
  rules will make your virtual discussions go more
  smoothly and be more enjoyable and productive.

Thank you for agreeing to lead your group in this study
of *Incarnation*. May it enrich your Advent and Christmas
season with a deeper appreciation of and desire to respond
to the mystery of the Son of God, made flesh for us!

SESSION 1

PRESIDENTS AND KINGS

Session Objectives

This session's readings, reflections, activities, and prayers will equip participants to

- discuss their understanding of what it means to call Jesus *King*;
- define the concepts of the Davidic Covenant and the messianic hope, and explain how these concepts helped Jesus's first followers understand him;
- reflect on how Jesus's birth, life, death, and resurrection led his followers to believe he was the fulfilment of ancient messianic hopes; and
- identify a specific "sphere of influence" in which they can witness to Jesus's rule this Advent season.

13

Biblical Foundations

Now when the king was settled in his house, and the LORD had given him rest from all his enemies around him, the king said to the prophet Nathan, "See now, I am living in a house of cedar, but the ark of God stays in a tent." Nathan said to the king, "Go, do all that you have in mind; for the LORD is with you."

But that same night the word of the LORD came to Nathan: Go and tell my servant David: Thus says the LORD: Are you the one to build me a house to live in? I have not lived in a house since the day I brought up the people of Israel from Egypt to this day, but I have been moving about in a tent and a tabernacle. Wherever I have moved about among all the people of Israel, did I ever speak a word with any of the tribal leaders of Israel, whom I commanded to shepherd my people Israel, saying, "Why have you not built me a house of cedar?" Now therefore thus you shall say to my servant David: Thus says the LORD of hosts: I took you from the pasture, from following the sheep to be prince over my people Israel; and I have been with you wherever you went, and have cut off all your enemies from before you; and I will make for you a great name, like the name of the great ones of the earth. And I will appoint a place for my people Israel and will plant them, so that they may live in their own place, and be disturbed no more; and evildoers shall afflict them no more, as formerly, from

*the time that I appointed judges over my people
Israel; and I will give you rest from all your
enemies. Moreover the* LORD *declares to you
that the* LORD *will make you a house. When
your days are fulfilled and you lie down with
your ancestors, I will raise up your offspring
after you, who shall come forth from your body,
and I will establish his kingdom. He shall build
a house for my name, and I will establish the
throne of his kingdom forever. I will be a father
to him, and he shall be a son to me. When he
commits iniquity, I will punish him with a rod
such as mortals use, with blows inflicted by
human beings. But I will not take my steadfast
love from him, as I took it from Saul, whom
I put away from before you. Your house and
your kingdom shall be made sure forever before
me; your throne shall be established forever.*

—2 Samuel 7:1-16

*In the sixth month the angel Gabriel was sent
by God to a town in Galilee called Nazareth,
to a virgin engaged to a man whose name was
Joseph, of the house of David. The virgin's
name was Mary. And he came to her and said,
"Greetings, favored one! The Lord is with you."
But she was much perplexed by his words and
pondered what sort of greeting this might be.
The angel said to her, "Do not be afraid, Mary,
for you have found favor with God. And now,
you will conceive in your womb and bear a
son, and you will name him Jesus. He will be
great, and will be called the Son of the Most
High, and the Lord God will give to him the*

*throne of his ancestor David. He will reign over
the house of Jacob forever, and of his kingdom
there will be no end." Mary said to the angel,
"How can this be, since I am a virgin?" The
angel said to her, "The Holy Spirit will come
upon you, and the power of the Most High
will overshadow you; therefore the child to be
born will be holy; he will be called Son of God.
And now, your relative Elizabeth in her old age
has also conceived a son; and this is the sixth
month for her who was said to be barren. For
nothing will be impossible with God." Then
Mary said, "Here am I, the servant of the Lord;
let it be with me according to your word." Then
the angel departed from her.*

—Luke 1:26-38

Leader Preparation

- Carefully read *Incarnation*, Chapter 1, as well as this session's Biblical Foundations, noting any topics you want or need to investigate further before the session. Consult trusted Bible dictionaries, concordances, and other resources as desired.
- Preview the DVD segment for this session.
- For this session you will need: *Incarnation* DVD; Bibles for participants who do not have their own; large sheets of paper or markerboard; hymnals (optional).

Starting Your Session

Welcome participants and talk about your interest in and enthusiasm for this group study of *Incarnation* by Adam Hamilton. Ask participants why they decided to join this study and what they hope to gain from it.

Use this icebreaker quiz to set the stage for this session. Ask participants to identify the presidential candidates (not all of whom won their elections) who used these campaign slogans. Bonus points if participants can identify the year![1]

- It's Morning in America Again (Ronald Reagan, 1984)
- Vote As You Shot (Ulysses S. Grant, 1868)
- Country First (John McCain, 2008)
- Yes, We Can (Barack Obama, 2008)
- He Kept Us Out of War (Woodrow Wilson, 1916)
- Happy Days Are Here Again (Franklin D. Roosevelt, 1932)
- In Your Heart, You Know He's Right (Barry Goldwater, 1964)
- Not Just Peanuts (Jimmy Carter, 1976)

Ask:

- Using just a few words, how would you describe the tone of the 2020 US presidential campaign?
- Adam Hamilton writes:

  "As much as we decry the polarization [of American politics], many of us participate in

---

1   https://www.mentalfloss.com/article/22920/10-memorable-presidential-campaign-slogans

it through our conversations and our use of social media." (page 17)

Do you agree with his assessment? Why or why not?

- How is a president like and unlike a king?
- What does it mean for you to call Jesus *king*? How meaningful do you find this title for him?

Read aloud from *Incarnation*:

"This season [of Advent] puts into perspective all our political wrangling; whatever Christians think about their president, and whoever we voted for in the various elections, we are meant to know that there is only one King. It is to him we give our highest allegiance." (page 17)

Tell participants this session will help your group explore both what Jesus's first followers meant when they called him *King*, and how—if at all—calling Jesus *King* can help us grow in faith and obedience today.

Pray this prayer or one of your own:

God Most High, who rules over all, you claim and call us all—despite our differences and disagreements—to be your Son's followers. May your Spirit so fill our minds and hearts in this time of reading and reflection that we understand and embody more fully what it means to praise the King of kings and Prince of Peace, Jesus Christ. Amen.

DVD Viewing

Watch the DVD segment for Session 1. Invite participants to offer comments or ask questions. Ask:

- Adam Hamilton thinks Advent should be a season of unity for Christians. Do you or have you experienced Advent in this way? How?
- Hamilton reflects on the royal titles bestowed upon Jesus in the New Testament's Advent and Christmas stories. What do you think of when you think about royalty? How easily or often do you think of Jesus as royalty?
- Who in the twenty-firstt-century culture and society is considered to be "royalty" and why? How do these "royals" compare and contrast with Jesus?
- In the video, Hamilton mentions the sermon "That's My King," by S. M. Lockridge. You can find a three-minute clip from the section of the sermon quoted by Hamilton at https://www.youtube.com/watch?v=yzqTFNfeDnE. If you wish, pull up this video and play it for your group, so that they can hear the sermon in Lockridge's own voice. What part of Lockridge's description of Jesus resonates most deeply with you? How would you describe your king?

King David, God's Anointed One

Ask participants to name some ceremonies or rituals, in the church and/or the larger society, in which people are identified or "set aside" for a special function or purpose. (Responses might include such examples as a medical student's white-coat ceremony, a presidential inauguration, or the ordination and installation of ministers and other church leaders.)

Tell participants that anointing with oil was a ceremony in ancient Israel. Read aloud from *Incarnation*:

> *"Though prophets, priests, and holy furnishings were anointed [with oil], it is the role of king that became most closely associated with anointing in scripture. King Saul, King David, King Solomon, and those who followed after them were hailed as* messiah—*as the Lord's anointed."* (page 23)

Explain to participants that *Christ* is a title deriving from the Greek translation of the Hebrew *Messiah*, and shares the same meaning, "anointed one." According to Hamilton, "in its most common usage, [the word] was another way of saying, 'king'" (page 34).

Have participants turn in their Bibles to 2 Samuel 7. Recruit a volunteer to read aloud 2 Samuel 7:1-16. Ask:

- Why is David troubled by where the ark of God—the ark of the covenant, the box which housed the Ten Commandments and which ancient Israel viewed as the footstool of God's throne—is stored, and what does he want to do about it? What is your opinion of David's plan?
- How does God, through Nathan the prophet, respond to David's plan? What does God promise David, and why?

20

- God's promise to David "became known as the Davidic Covenant," writes Hamilton. "That promise had a profound impact upon the Jewish people, who found hope in it during long periods when they were living in exile or when foreign kings ruled over the land" (page 25). Why did this promise have such power to sustain them? What does that power suggest about how they remembered King David?

- What leaders, if any, from your congregation or community's past do you remember during difficult times? How do these memories sustain and motivate you?

- What dangers, if any, arise when people idealize their leaders from the past?

The Messianic Hope

Read aloud from *Incarnation*:

> *"This hope for an ideal king, like David, is what became known as the 'messianic hope.'"*

(page 26)

Form three small groups of participants and assign each group one of the following scriptures:

- Isaiah 9:2-7
- Jeremiah 23:1-8
- Ezekiel 34:23-31

Ask each group to read the assigned passage and discuss how it contributes to an understanding of the messianic hope. After sufficient time, have someone from each group share highlights of their group's discussions.

Jesus As the Messianic Hope Fulfilled

Have participants turn in their Bibles to Luke 1. Recruit volunteers to read aloud Luke 1:26-38, taking the "roles" of Mary, Gabriel, and the narrator. Ask:

- How do Gabriel's words about Jesus echo ancient messianic hopes? How do you imagine Mary, a devout Jew, felt about the angel's words?
- Based on our discussion so far of messianic hope and what you know of Jesus's ministry, why did Jesus's followers come to believe he fulfilled that hope?
- Adam Hamilton describes Jesus's public ministry as "his campaign for the office of King" (page 30). How helpful do you find this metaphor for Jesus's work and why?
- "Just as Jesus's campaign was not what we'd expect from one seeking to rule," writes Hamilton, "his anointing and coronation were likewise out of the ordinary" (page 34). Read Luke 7:36-50 and John 19:1-22. How do these scriptures about Jesus's "anointing" and "coronation" show what Jesus thought it meant to be king?
- How did Jesus's resurrection on Easter validate his status as King for his followers?
- Hamilton cites Revelation 19:11-12, 16 as one vision of Jesus's "triumphant return" as king, when his rule will break the world fully and finally. What does Revelation's imagery make you think and feel about Jesus's kingship? How consistent do you think Revelation's vision of Jesus as King is with

the nature of Jesus's kingship as seen in his life
and ministry? Why?

- Hamilton writes,

  *"[T]hough we live in that time between
  triumphs, the triumph of [Jesus's] Resurrection
  and that of the Second Coming, the first gives
  us confidence in the second."* (page 39)

  How confident do you feel this Advent season in
  Jesus's ultimate triumph as *King*? Why?

Closing Your Session

Ask:

- Hamilton writes,

  *"I don't believe it is an overstatement to say
  that [Jesus] is the single most influential
  person to have walked this planet."* (page 39)

  Do you agree? Why or why not?
- How important, if at all, do you think it is for
  modern Christians to continue calling Jesus
  King? Why?
- What other titles or images, if any, would help
  people today understand Jesus in the way the title
  King does?

Read aloud from *Incarnation*:

  *"I don't know your politics, but if you are a
  Christian, I know your King. His Sermon
  on the Mount, his parables, and his great
  commandments calling us to love God and
  neighbor represent the laws of his kingdom.*

Our allegiance to him comes above all other allegiances." (pages 41–42)

Invite participants to write down a specific place or relationship—in which they do or could witness to Jesus's rule, and one specific way they could do so this Advent season. Consider asking volunteers to talk briefly about their responses (be prepared to do so yourself).

Close the session using the prayer at the end of *Incarnation*, Chapter 1; with the prayer below; or with one of your own.

Eternal God, through the ages your people have longed for a righteous ruler who will speed up the day your will is finally done on earth as in heaven. In Jesus, your Anointed One, you anointed us to do your will as citizens of your kingdom. By your Spirit, keep us strong and hopeful as his faithful and obedient subjects. Amen.

Optional Extension

Distribute hymnals and look for Advent and Christmas hymns and carols that use royal titles and images for Jesus. (For more of a challenge, ask participants to remember all the royal language from the songs of the season they can!) In addition to (or instead of) the closing prayer above, close your session by singing one of these songs together.

SESSION 2

THE SAVIOR AND OUR NEED FOR SAVING

Session Objectives

This session's readings, reflections, activities, and prayers will equip participants to

- describe the significance of what Jesus's name means in the context of New Testament stories about his birth;
- articulate their understandings of sin and consider how the story of Eve, Adam, and the serpent in Genesis 3 shapes those understandings;
- explore two major ways in which scripture explains how Jesus saves us from sin; and
- contemplate how Jesus *has saved*, *is saving*, and *will yet save* them.

Biblical Foundations

Now the birth of Jesus the Messiah took place in this way. When his mother Mary had been engaged to Joseph, but before they lived together, she was found to be with child from the Holy Spirit. Her husband Joseph, being a righteous man and unwilling to expose her to public disgrace, planned to dismiss her quietly. But just when he had resolved to do this, an angel of the Lord appeared to him in a dream and said, "Joseph, son of David, do not be afraid to take Mary as your wife, for the child conceived in her is from the Holy Spirit. She will bear a son, and you are to name him Jesus, for he will save his people from their sins."
—Matthew 1:18-21

In that region there were shepherds living in the fields, keeping watch over their flock by night. Then an angel of the Lord stood before them, and the glory of the Lord shone around them, and they were terrified. But the angel said to them, "Do not be afraid; for see—I am bringing you good news of great joy for all the people: to you is born this day in the city of David a Savior, who is the Messiah, the Lord. This will be a sign for you: you will find a child wrapped in bands of cloth and lying in a manger." And suddenly there was with the angel a multitude of the heavenly host, praising God and saying,

> *"Glory to God in the highest heaven,*
> *and on earth peace among those whom he favors!"*

—Luke 2:8-14

*Now the serpent was more crafty than any
other wild animal that the Lord God had made.
He said to the woman, "Did God say, 'You
shall not eat from any tree in the garden'?"
The woman said to the serpent, "We may eat
of the fruit of the trees in the garden; but God
said, 'You shall not eat of the fruit of the tree
that is in the middle of the garden, nor shall
you touch it, or you shall die.'" But the serpent
said to the woman, "You will not die; for God
knows that when you eat of it your eyes will
be opened, and you will be like God, knowing
good and evil." So when the woman saw that
the tree was good for food, and that it was a
delight to the eyes, and that the tree was to
be desired to make one wise, she took of its
fruit and ate; and she also gave some to her
husband, who was with her, and he ate.
Then the eyes of both were opened, and they
knew that they were naked; and they sewed
fig leaves together and made loincloths for
themselves.*

*They heard the sound of the Lord God walking
in the garden at the time of the evening breeze,
and the man and his wife hid themselves from
the presence of the Lord God among the trees of
the garden. But the Lord God called to the man,
and said to him, "Where are you?" He said,
"I heard the sound of you in the garden, and
I was afraid, because I was naked; and I hid
myself." He said, "Who told you that you were
naked? Have you eaten from the tree of which*

I commanded you not to eat?" The man said,
"The woman whom you gave to be with me,
she gave me fruit from the tree, and I ate." Then
the LORD God said to the woman, "What is this
that you have done?" The woman said, "The
serpent tricked me, and I ate."

—Genesis 3:1-13

For I know that nothing good dwells within
me, that is, in my flesh. I can will what is right,
but I cannot do it. For I do not do the good I
want, but the evil I do not want is what I do.
Now if I do what I do not want, it is no longer
I that do it, but sin that dwells within me.

So I find it to be a law that when I want to do
what is good, evil lies close at hand. For I delight in the law of God in my inmost self, but I
see in my members another law at war with the
law of my mind, making me captive to the law
of sin that dwells in my members. Wretched
man that I am! Who will rescue me from this
body of death? Thanks be to God through Jesus
Christ our Lord!

So then, with my mind I am a slave to the law
of God, but with my flesh I am a slave to the
law of sin.

—Romans 7:18-25

Leader Preparation

- Carefully read *Incarnation*, Chapter 2, as well
  as this session's Biblical Foundations, noting

any topics you want or need to investigate further before the session. Consult trusted Bible dictionaries, concordances, and other resources as desired.

- Preview the DVD segment for this session.
- For this session you will need: *Incarnation* DVD; Bibles for participants who do not have their own; large sheets of paper or markerboard; newspapers and magazines (optional).
- Before the session, write the list of scripture passages in the section titled "How Does Jesus Save?" on large sheets of paper or markerboard, leaving space for writing notes about each one.

Starting Your Session

Welcome participants. Ask those who attended the previous session to talk briefly about what they found most interesting, encouraging, or challenging from it, and how it affected their relationship with Jesus and others.

Ask:

- What is your name's meaning and origin?
- Why and how you were given your name?
- Have you ever wanted to change your name? If so, what would you change it to and why?

Ask if any participants know what Jesus's name means (some likely will). Read aloud from *Incarnation*:

> "Jesus *is an anglicized version of the Greek version of his name. But the [original] Hebrew is* Yeshua, *a shortened version of* Yehoshua.

*It comes from the personal name for God in
Hebrew,* Yahweh, *and the word for 'to save' or
'to deliver,'* yasha. Yeshua *therefore means 'God
saves,' 'God delivers,' or 'God helps.'"* (page 48)

Tell participants that Session 2 explores the significance
of what Jesus's name means and why it is appropriate
for him.

Pray this prayer or one of your own:

*Holy and righteous God, before you we can only admit our
own unrighteousness and our world's deep brokenness. In
gratitude, we praise you for giving your Son. In humility, we
pray you will guide us now, by your Spirit, to live more fully
and freely as his forgiven people. Amen.*

DVD Viewing

Watch the DVD segment for Session 2. Invite participants to offer comments or ask questions. Ask:

- Adam Hamilton notes the Advent and Christmas
  stories in scripture call Jesus "Savior." In
  your opinion, how prominently do Christmas
  celebrations in the church and in our culture
  focus on Jesus's identity as Savior?
- Hamilton points out that some Christians find
  language of "being saved" uncomfortable. How
  do you respond to talk of "being saved" and
  why?
- Hamilton believes affirming Jesus as Savior
  means, in large part, affirming that we and
  other people are loved and accepted by God.
  Who do you know, this holiday season, who

needs to hear God loves and accepts them? What specific actions could you take to share with them the good news of Jesus as Savior?

Jesus's Name in Stories of His Birth

Have participants turn in their Bibles to Matthew 1. Recruit a volunteer to read aloud Matthew 1:18-21. Ask:

- Why does the angel tell Joseph to name Mary's child *Jesus*?
- Adam Hamilton writes, "There's a little naughtiness in us all," (page 47) yet Matthew calls Joseph "a righteous man." How does this story illustrate Joseph's righteousness? By what criteria do we recognize righteous people today?
- The angel says Jesus will save "his people." Who were and are Jesus's people?
- Do righteous people like Joseph need to be saved from sins? Why or why not?

Have participants turn to Luke 2. Recruit a volunteer to read aloud Luke 2:8-13; have your entire group read verse 14 (the angels' praise) aloud in unison. Ask:

- For whom is Jesus's birth "good news of great joy," both then and now?
- How does the angel's message to the shepherds echo the ancient messianic hopes discussed in Session 1? How do these echoes shape our expectation of what it means to call Jesus *Savior*?
- Luke's story of Jesus's birth implicitly contrasts its central characters—the infant Jesus, his

parents, and the shepherds—with people who represent military and economic power (see 2:1-2). Why might people without privilege and status especially welcome a Savior's birth as good news?

Missing the Mark

Optional: Distribute newspapers and magazines. Ask participants to find an image of sin. Invite volunteers to talk about why they chose the image they did.

Read aloud from *Incarnation*:

> *"In both the Old and the New Testaments, the words most commonly translated as sin... mean to stray from the path or to miss the mark.... we're meant to follow as human beings."* (page 52)

Invite responses to this definition and image.

Ask participants how they would answer the woman who asked Adam Hamilton, "Why do Christians spend so much time talking about sin?" (page 51). After discussion, read aloud from *Incarnation*:

> *"The good news of Jesus is not that we're sinners, but that he is our Savior. But we can't appreciate his role as Savior if we don't know we need to be saved!"* (page 52)

Have participants turn in their Bibles to Genesis. Recruit volunteers to read aloud Genesis 3:1-13, taking the "roles" of the narrator, the serpent, the woman, the man, and God. Ask:

- How is this a story about "straying from the path" or "missing the mark"?
- "The story is not intended to teach us ancient history," writes Hamilton, but "to teach us about ourselves" (page 55). Do you agree? Why or why not?
- "[W]hen the Bible speaks of sin," Hamilton writes, "it means both the innate *tendency to stray* from the right path and also the *act of straying*" (page 54). Do you tend to think of sin as individuals' wrong acts or as an external, larger problem in humanity and the world? What are the risks of thinking about sin in only one way or the other?
- Discuss these questions from *Incarnation*:

  "What is the forbidden fruit the serpent beckons you to eat? The lie he tells you to lead you astray or to trip you up? Where do you stray from the path or miss the mark?" (page 55)

How Jesus Saves

Have participants turn in their Bibles to Romans. Recruit a volunteer to read aloud Romans 7:18-25. Ask:

- What is the conflict Paul describes?
- When, if ever, have you experienced this struggle yourself?
- Do you believe "nothing good dwells within" us? Why or why not?
- Paul calls his body a "body of death." Is the human body inherently sinful? Why or why not?

Tell participants that although Christians believe Jesus saves us from sin, as Paul writes, Christians understand exactly *how* Jesus saves us in different ways.

Read aloud from *Incarnation* Adam Hamilton's descriptions of two different understandings of how Jesus saves us from sin:

> *"Some see his redemptive work mechanistically, transactionally, or juridically: Jesus, God in the flesh, the one holy and righteous man who ever lived, died in our place for our sins.... [H]is death was a full and sufficient payment....*
>
> *Others see Jesus's death on the cross...less in transactional terms and more in terms of God's attempt to speak to us about sin, mercy, and love."* (page 63)

Explain that scripture supports both these views (and others) of how Jesus saves us. Recruit volunteers to read aloud each of the scriptures on the list below (which you wrote on large sheets of paper or markerboard before the session). After each reading, ask participants whether they think the scripture supports one view more than the other, both, or neither. Write notes as participants discuss. Expect (and, to the extent you and your group would be comfortable, encourage) civil disagreement!

- John 15:12-13
- Romans 3:21-26
- Romans 5:6-11
- 2 Corinthians 5:14-21
- 1 John 2:1-2
- 1 Peter 2:21-25

Ask:

- Which of the two understandings of Jesus's saving work that Hamilton discusses appeals to you the most and why? If they appeal to you equally or neither appeals to you, why?
- Why does scripture explain how Jesus saves in a variety of ways and picture it with a variety of images?
- How should this variety shape what we believe and say about how Jesus saves within the church? To those outside the church?
- Hamilton also explores how Jesus saves us from "existential crisis"—those "moments when we question the meaning of our existence" (page 67). When, if ever, have you experienced Jesus's power to save in such a moment?
- Hamilton identifies death 0as "the greatest existential crisis" (page 76 from which Jesus saves us. How does Jesus's death and resurrection change your perspective on death—your own death someday or the loss of those for whom you've mourned?

Closing Your Session

In this chapter, Adam Hamilton mentions three "senses and tenses" in which the New Testament speaks of Jesus saving us: Jesus *has* saved us (past tense), Jesus *is* saving us (present tense), and Jesus *will* save us (future tense).

Have participants divide an index card or piece of scrap paper into three columns. Invite them to write (or draw) a response, one per column, to each of these prompts:

- Jesus has saved me from...
- Jesus is saving me from...
- Jesus will save me from...

Consider asking volunteers to talk briefly about their responses (be prepared to do so yourself).

Close the session using the prayer at the end of *Incarnation*, Chapter 2 or by singing or reading aloud together one of the Christmas hymns by Christina Rossetti that Hamilton discusses in Chapter 2, available in many hymnals or online: "Love Came Down at Christmas" (https://hymnary.org/text/love_came_down_at_christmas) and "In the Bleak Midwinter" (https://hymnary.org/text/in_the_bleak_midwinter). You might also try searching YouTube or other websites for video recordings of these hymns.

Optional Extensions

1. When discussing the definition of "sin," set up a simple "target practice" activity for your group (for example, throwing wadded-up newspaper into a recycling bin from across the room, or a toy bow and suction-cup arrow game). Play the game and discuss how difficult "hitting the mark" consistently can be.

2. Find various musical settings of the angelic praise in Luke 2:14 and listen to them as a group. How does the music affect participants' "great joy" about the birth of a Savior?

SESSION 3

EMMANUEL IN THE MIDST OF A PANDEMIC

Session Objectives

This session's readings, reflections, activities, and prayers will equip participants to

- understand what Isaiah's prophecy about *Immanuel* meant in its original context;
- appreciate why early Christians like Matthew found new meaning in Isaiah's prophecy when reflecting on their experience of Jesus;
- reflect on theological questions raised in the doctrine of the Incarnation;
- articulate the practical benefits of the Incarnation, guided by passages from Hebrews; and
- identify images of "putting flesh on" God's love that can inspire them to similar action.

Biblical Foundations

All this took place to fulfill what had been spoken by the Lord through the prophet:

> *"Look, the virgin shall conceive and bear
> a son,
>   and they shall name him Emmanuel,"*

which means, "God is with us." When Joseph awoke from sleep, he did as the angel of the Lord commanded him; he took her as his wife, but had no marital relations with her until she had borne a son; and he named him Jesus.
> —Matthew 1:22-25

In the days of Ahaz son of Jotham son of Uzziah, king of Judah, King Rezin of Aram and King Pekah son of Remaliah of Israel went up to attack Jerusalem, but could not mount an attack against it. When the house of David heard that Aram had allied itself with Ephraim, the heart of Ahaz and the heart of his people shook as the trees of the forest shake before the wind.

Then the LORD said to Isaiah, Go out to meet Ahaz, you and your son Shear-jashub, at the end of the conduit of the upper pool on the highway to the Fuller's Field, and say to him, Take heed, be quiet, do not fear, and do not let your heart be faint because of these two smoldering stumps of firebrands, because of the fierce anger of Rezin and Aram and the son of Remaliah. Because Aram—with Ephraim and

the son of Remaliah—has plotted evil against
you, saying, Let us go up against Judah and cut
off Jerusalem and conquer it for ourselves and
make the son of Tabeel king in it; therefore thus
says the Lord GOD:

> It shall not stand,
>> and it shall not come to pass.

> For the head of Aram is Damascus,
>> and the head of Damascus is Rezin.

(Within sixty-five years Ephraim will be
shattered, no longer a people.)

> The head of Ephraim is Samaria,
>> and the head of Samaria is the son of
>> Remaliah.

> If you do not stand firm in faith,
>> you shall not stand at all.

Again the LORD spoke to Ahaz, saying, Ask a
sign of the LORD your God; let it be deep as
Sheol or high as heaven. But Ahaz said, I will
not ask, and I will not put the LORD to the
test. Then Isaiah said: "Hear then, O house of
David! Is it too little for you to weary mortals,
that you weary my God also? Therefore the
Lord himself will give you a sign. Look, the
young woman is with child and shall bear a
son, and shall name him Immanuel. He shall
eat curds and honey by the time he knows how
to refuse the evil and choose the good. For
before the child knows how to refuse the evil

*and choose the good, the land before whose two
kings you are in dread will be deserted."*

Isaiah 7:1-16

*Long ago God spoke to our ancestors in many
and various ways by the prophets, but in these
last days he has spoken to us by a Son, whom
he appointed heir of all things, through whom
he also created the worlds. He is the reflection
of God's glory and the exact imprint of God's
very being, and he sustains all things by his
powerful word. When he had made purifica-
tion for sins, he sat down at the right hand of
the Majesty on high, having become as much
superior to angels as the name he has inherited
is more excellent than theirs....*

*Since, then, we have a great high priest who
has passed through the heavens, Jesus, the Son
of God, let us hold fast to our confession. For
we do not have a high priest who is unable to
sympathize with our weaknesses, but we have
one who in every respect has been tested as we
are, yet without sin. Let us therefore approach
the throne of grace with boldness, so that we
may receive mercy and find grace to help in
time of need.*

—Hebrews 1:1-4; 4:14-16

Leader Preparation

- Carefully read *Incarnation*, Chapter 3, as well
  as this session's Biblical Foundations, noting
  any topics you want or need to investigate

further before the session. Consult trusted Bible dictionaries, concordances, and other resources as desired.

- Preview the DVD segment for this session.
- For this session you will need: *Incarnation* DVD; Bibles for participants who do not have their own; large sheets of paper or markerboard; newspapers and magazines.

Starting Your Session

Welcome participants. Ask those who attended the previous session to talk briefly about what they found most interesting, encouraging, or challenging from it, and how it affected their relationship with Jesus and others.

Invite participants to think and talk about ways the Advent and Christmas seasons of 2020 are (or were, if your group is using this study in later years) different because of the COVID-19 pandemic. Responses may range from objectively small alterations to holiday traditions to marking the holidays while dealing with lost employment, personal health, or loved ones. Acknowledge all contributions to the discussion, modeling acceptance of and respect for participants' emotions.

Tell participants Adam Hamilton wrote Chapter 3 of *Incarnation* during the early days of the pandemic's height in the US. Read aloud from the book:

> *"I'm writing... knowing things may get worse before they get better. I sit here bracing for what lies ahead, but I do so with hope—a hope that is rooted in Advent and Christmas."*

> (pages 90–91)

Explain that this session explores how the message of Emmanuel—"God with us"—was a message of hope at times of sadness, doubt, and fear in both the Old and New Testaments, and whether it can still be a message of hope in similar times today.

Pray this prayer or one of your own:

Who is like you, God Most High, drawing near to those who are low and in need to raise them up? In your Son Jesus, you entered human life for a time, that we might forever enter yours. May we sense you near us even now, through your Spirit, that we may take heart in our darkest and most fearful times, trusting that you abide with us, our Lord Emmanuel. Amen.

DVD Viewing

Watch the DVD segment for Session 3. Invite participants to offer comments or ask questions. Ask:

- Adam Hamilton shares his memories of and feelings about the earliest effects of the COVID-19 pandemic in the US. What do you remember most about that time?
- Hamilton doesn't think God caused the pandemic, but that God brought good out of it, and was with us through it (and continues to be with us). Do you agree? Why or why not?
- Why does Hamilton think the message of *Emmanuel* is one people living in times of fear need to hear?

Finding a New Meaning in an Old Prophecy

Ask volunteers to talk about a time they found different or additional meanings in a song, poem, story, or artwork with which they had long been familiar. Ask:

- What prompted your new appreciations and understandings?
- Did these new or extra meanings invalidate ones you previously had? Why or why not?

Explain that Matthew, in his account of Jesus's birth, calls Jesus *Emmanuel* because Jesus's followers found new and additional meanings in the Book of Isaiah. Read aloud from *Incarnation*:

> *"Much of what Isaiah prophesied was…*
> *addressing the specific circumstances of the*
> *prophet's day or the near future.… But every*
> *generation of Jews that followed Isaiah's time*
> *looked at his words in light of their own time,*
> *and heard in them a picture of how God might*
> *work in their time as well."* (page 98)

Read or review the historical background to Isaiah 7 found in the Chapter 3 (in the section titled "Isaiah's Prophecy"). Recruit a volunteer to read aloud Isaiah 7:1-9. (Assure your volunteer no one will be grading their pronunciation of difficult names!) Ask:

- Why were King Ahaz and his subjects feeling afraid?

- Why does Isaiah compare the enemy kings to smoldering stumps (verse 4)?
- How is the name of Isaiah's son, Shear-jashub ("a remnant shall return"), meant to be a message of hope for Ahaz?
- Isaiah urges Ahaz to rely on God and not on military allies, telling him, "If you do not stand firm in faith, you shall not stand at all" (verse 9). When you feel afraid, who or what are you tempted to rely on rather than God? What does "standing firm in faith" look like practically in times of fear and panic? How do we find strength to do so?

Recruit a volunteer to read aloud Isaiah 7:10-16. Ask:

- Other scriptures warn against testing God (Deuteronomy 6:16; Matthew 4:7). What makes Ahaz's refusal to test God a sign of fear, not faith?
- What sign does God promise through Isaiah and how is it meant to address Ahaz's fear?
- How does the name of the child who will be born underscore his birth as a reason not to fear?

Recruit a volunteer to read aloud Matthew 1:22-25. Ask:

- What new and different meaning does Matthew find in Isaiah's centuries-old message for King Ahaz?
- Why might Joseph have been feeling afraid (refer back to Matthew 1:18-21)?
- Matthew, a Jew who wrote in Greek, used the Greek translation of Isaiah, which is why 2:23

speaks of a "virgin" while Isaiah 7:14 speaks of a "young woman." Does this difference in translation affect your beliefs about Jesus's birth? Why or why not?

- Matthew describes Jesus's birth as a profound fulfillment of Isaiah's words. Does identifying Jesus as Emmanuel add to, take away from, or not affect the importance of the sign God gave King Ahaz? Why?

Contemplation of the Incarnation

Read aloud from *Incarnation*:

> *"Matthew alone found in this somewhat obscure verse [Isaiah 7:14] a powerful picture of who Jesus is and why he came. The emphasis on Jesus's conception by the Holy Spirit seems to be Matthew's way of pointing to his unique identity.... somehow [to be] both Son of Man and Son of God."* (pages 100–101)

Tell participants Hamilton is summarizing the classic doctrine (teaching) of the Incarnation: in Jesus, the essential nature of God became one of us.

Ask:

- What are some helpful and/or unhelpful ways you have heard the Incarnation explained—or perhaps have even used yourself to explain it?
- As Hamilton points out, Matthew "does not offer us a fully developed Trinitarian theology of how God is at once Father, Son, and Holy Spirit" (page

101) (nor does any other New Testament author). The word *Trinity* doesn't appear in the Bible. What Matthew (like other New Testament authors) *does* offer is evidence of how Jesus's first followers experienced and responded to him. What biblical evidence of people's experiences of Jesus can you think of that point to Jesus's humanity? To his divinity?

- How would you respond to someone who says, "If the Bible doesn't teach the Trinity, I can't believe it"?

- Christianity teaches "that God in Jesus did not simply assume human appearance," writes Hamilton, "but…actually was born and lived as a human being" (page 106). By the fourth century, the church officially rejected the idea that Jesus only seemed human. What's the difference between a Jesus who *appears* human and a Jesus who *is* human? What's at stake?

- What things in life do you find mysterious yet still trust are true? Why? How are these things like and/or unlike the mystery of the Incarnation?

Seeing the Son of God in Hebrews

Have participants turn in their Bibles to Hebrews. Recruit one volunteer to read aloud Hebrews 1:1-4. Ask:

- What, specifically, does the author of Hebrews mean by calling Jesus *God's Son*? Why does Jesus's identity as God's Son matter to us, according to these verses?

- How does Jesus, God's Son, allow us to see God? What distinguishes him from idols?

Recruit another volunteer to read aloud Hebrews 4:14-16. Ask:

- Why does Jesus's status as Son of God matter to us, according to these verses?
- In your personal faith, do you tend to think of God as distant and judgmental, or as approachable and sympathetic to you? Why?
- How do you respond to the idea that, because of the Incarnation, God is, as Hamilton writes, a God who has "experienced what we experience as humans. In Jesus, God experienced temptation, love, hunger, joy, fear, friendship, grief, doubt, rejection, a sense of abandonment by God, and death"? (page 102)

Closing Your Session

Read aloud from *Incarnation*:

> "As Emmanuel, [Jesus] seeks to remind you
> that he is always with you and you don't need
> to be afraid. He calls you to go in his name to
> incarnate God's love to others." (page 114)

Distribute newspapers and magazines. Ask participants to look for pictures of one person showing love to others in ways that remind participants of God's love, as given flesh in Jesus's life. Invite volunteers to explain why they chose the pictures they did. Ask:

- How do these pictures inspire you to "put flesh on" God's love for others this Advent and Christmas season, especially those living in sadness, doubt, and fear?

Optional: Hamilton anticipates his readers will know stories of people who've cared for persons with COVID-19 in ways that incarnate God's love. Invite participants to talk about such experiences from their own or others' experiences.

Close the session using the prayer at the end of *Incarnation*, Chapter 3; with the prayer below; or with one of your own.

Jesus our Emmanuel, you came among us as one of us, and you promise to be with us always, transforming us to be more like you. By your grace, may others know through what we do that God is with them. Amen.

Optional Extensions

1. In Chapter 3, Hamilton mentions the song "One of Us" (1995, written by Eric Bazilian, first recorded by Joan Osborne): "To me it's a Christmas carol, capturing the essence of the Christian gospel" (page 105). Listen to the song and read and discuss its lyrics together. Do you agree with Hamilton's assessment of it? Why or why not?

2. In Chapter 3, Hamilton mentions the comedies *Oh, God!* (1977) and *Bruce Almighty* (2003). If your group is interested, arrange a time to watch one of these films together. Compare and contrast the movie's ideas about God being with human beings versus Christian belief in the Incarnation.

SESSION 4

LIGHT OF THE WORLD, WORD OF GOD, AND LORD

Session Objectives

This session's readings, reflections, activities, and prayers will equip participants to

- understand the Gospel of John's identification of Jesus as God's Word and God's light;
- examine the prophet Isaiah's call for righteous living that shines God's light in a dark world; and
- contemplate how the magi's visit to the young Jesus points to Jesus as Lord.

Biblical Foundations

In the beginning was the Word, and the Word was with God, and the Word was God. He was in the beginning with God. All things came into

*being through him, and without him not one
thing came into being. What has come into
being in him was life, and the life was the light
of all people. The light shines in the darkness,
and the darkness did not overcome it....*

*The true light, which enlightens everyone, was
coming into the world.*

*He was in the world, and the world came into
being through him; yet the world did not know
him. He came to what was his own, and his
own people did not accept him. But to all who
received him, who believed in his name, he
gave power to become children of God, who
were born, not of blood or of the will of the
flesh or of the will of man, but of God.*

*And the Word became flesh and lived among
us, and we have seen his glory, the glory as of a
father's only son, full of grace and truth.*
                                    —John 1:1-5, 9-14

> *Shout out, do not hold back!*
> > *Lift up your voice like a trumpet!*
>
> *Announce to my people their rebellion,*
> > *to the house of Jacob their sins.*
>
> *Yet day after day they seek me*
> > *and delight to know my ways,*
>
> *as if they were a nation that practiced
> righteousness*
> > *and did not forsake the ordinance of
> > their God;*

they ask of me righteous judgments,
  they delight to draw near to God.

"Why do we fast, but you do not see?
  Why humble ourselves, but you do not
  notice?"

Look, you serve your own interest on your
fast day,
  and oppress all your workers.

Look, you fast only to quarrel and to fight
  and to strike with a wicked fist.

Such fasting as you do today
  will not make your voice heard on high.

Is such the fast that I choose,
  a day to humble oneself?

Is it to bow down the head like a bulrush,
  and to lie in sackcloth and ashes?

Will you call this a fast,
  a day acceptable to the LORD?

Is not this the fast that I choose:
  to loose the bonds of injustice,

  to undo the thongs of the yoke,

to let the oppressed go free,
  and to break every yoke?

Is it not to share your bread with the
hungry,
  and bring the homeless poor into your
  house;

when you see the naked, to cover them,
and not to hide yourself from your
own kin?

Then your light shall break forth like
the dawn,
and your healing shall spring up
quickly;

your vindicator shall go before you,
the glory of the LORD shall be your rear
guard.

Then you shall call, and the LORD will
answer;
you shall cry for help, and he will say,
Here I am.

If you remove the yoke from among you,
the pointing of the finger, the speaking
of evil,

If you offer your food to the hungry
and satisfy the needs of the afflicted,

then your light shall rise in the darkness
and your gloom be like the noonday.

—Isaiah 58:1-10

Then Herod secretly called for the wise men and
learned from them the exact time when the star
had appeared. Then he sent them to Bethlehem,
saying, "Go and search diligently for the child;
and when you have found him, bring me word
so that I may also go and pay him homage."
When they had heard the king, they set out; and

*there, ahead of them, went the star that they
had seen at its rising, until it stopped over the
place where the child was. When they saw that
the star had stopped, they were overwhelmed
with joy. On entering the house, they saw the
child with Mary his mother; and they knelt
down and paid him homage. Then, opening
their treasure chests, they offered him gifts of
gold, frankincense, and myrrh. And having
been warned in a dream not to return to Herod,
they left for their own country by another road.*
—Matthew 2:7-12

*[Jesus said,] "You are the light of the world. A
city built on a hill cannot be hid. No one after
lighting a lamp puts it under the bushel basket,
but on the lampstand, and it gives light to all in
the house. In the same way, let your light shine
before others, so that they may see your good
works and give glory to your Father in heaven."*
—Matthew 5:14-16

Leader Preparation

- Carefully read Chapter 4 and the Epilogue of
  Incarnation, as well as this session's Biblical
  Foundations, noting any topics you want or need
  to investigate further before the session. Consult
  trusted Bible dictionaries, concordances, and
  other resources as desired.
- Preview the DVD segment for this session.
- For this session you will need: *Incarnation* DVD;
  Bibles for participants who do not have their
  own; large sheets of paper or markerboard; one

53

large wax or electric candle; and enough smaller candles or electric votives for each participant to use one.

Starting Your Session

Welcome participants. Ask those who attended the previous session to talk briefly about what they found most interesting, encouraging, or challenging from it, and how it affected their relationship with Jesus and others.

Darken your meeting space as much as possible, then light the large candle or electric votive. Invite participants to speak aloud words or brief phrases expressing their thoughts, feelings, or other reactions to seeing a light in the darkness. Ask participants not to comment on one another's responses. Be sensitive toward participants with vision impairments who may experience this activity differently from others.

When you feel all who are going to respond have responded, tell participants this final session of your study will explore three more titles for Jesus from the Bible's Christmas stories, including the title "Light of the world."

Pray this prayer or one of your own:

Creator God, in the beginning you called light from darkness, and you have made your light to shine in our hearts by displaying your glory in the person of Jesus Christ. In his light, may our spirits see light in this time together, that we may not only honor you as we celebrate the coming of your light but also serve you as we carry your light, in the power of your Spirit, to a world in darkness. Amen.

Extinguish or turn off the large candle and restore normal lighting before continuing.

DVD Viewing

Watch the DVD segment for Session 4. Invite participants to offer comments or ask questions. Ask:

- Adam Hamilton talks about the Christmas candlelight service he leads each year. How does your congregation use candles in its Advent and Christmas worship? How do you use candles or other lights in your own or your family's Christmas traditions?
- Hamilton mentions some memorable instances of light in scripture. What others can you think of? What connections, if any, can you draw between them and the Christmas message?
- Hamilton reminds us Christmas is, on the traditional Christian calendar, a season continuing until the feast of Epiphany (January 6). In Western Christianity, Epiphany commemorates the wise men's visit to the child Jesus. How, if at all, does your congregation celebrate Epiphany? How do the wise men figure in your own holiday celebrations? What do they represent for you?

John's "Christmas Story"

Have participants turn in their Bibles to John 1. Read aloud from *Incarnation*:

*"Absent [from John] are the stories of Mary
and Joseph. There's no journey to Bethlehem,
no shepherds, no wise men, no birth in a
stable—but my, how rich is John's account of
Christmas." (page 121)*

Recruit one volunteer to read aloud John 1:1-5 and
another to read John 1:9-14. Ask:

- Why does Hamilton call these verses "John's
  account of Christmas"? (page 121)
- In what ways are these verses also John's account
  of Creation?
- John claims God's Word became a human being
  in Jesus (verses 1, 14). The Greek word for
  word is "logos." "[L]ogos, which means word,"
  writes Hamilton, "also has the connotation of
  reasoning, wisdom, or logic" (page 133). What
  do these definitions tell you about who John
  says Jesus is? What does thinking of Jesus as the
  Word of God mean to you?
- Hamilton notes,

  *"While Christians often speak about the Bible
  as the Word of God, the Word of God in its
  most decisive and definitive form came to us
  not as a book, but as a person." (page 134)*

  If Jesus is the Word of God, should Christians
  also refer to scripture as the Word of God?
  Why or why not?
- John states not everyone welcomed God's Word,
  God's light (verses 9-13; compare John 3:19-21).
  How do you believe God's Word is rejected today?

When have you rejected or resisted God's Word and light?

- "Christmas," writes Hamilton, "is God's response to both forms of darkness, the moral and the existential" (page 127). How do you respond to John's claim that darkness does not overcome God's light (verse 5)?

Called to Spread the Light of God

Read aloud from *Incarnation*:

> *"As we become children of the light, we cannot keep that light within ourselves. It is meant to spill out from us naturally and touch the lives of others.... What does carrying light into the dark places look like? Centuries before Jesus, Isaiah the prophet pointed the people of Israel toward an answer."* (pages 141–142)

Have participants turn in their Bibles to Isaiah 58. Recruit volunteers to read aloud Isaiah 58:1-10. Ask:

- What problem does this prophecy address? What connections, if any, do you draw between this ancient condemnation of the people's worship and modern celebrations, in society and church, of Christmas today?
- How does God promise the people can experience light instead of darkness? What implications does God's promise hold for church and society today?

57

- This prophecy describes the "fast" God chooses. From what must God's people fast in order to do what God wants them to do?
- How, specifically, is your congregation involved in the work to which God calls the people in this prophecy?
- Hamilton writes that we sometimes ask why God hasn't done something about the darkness in our world, but God answers, "I did do something. I sent Jesus to be the light so you could see what to do" (page 140). How satisfying or unsatisfying do you find this answer, and why?

Kneeling Before the Lord

Have participants turn in their Bibles to Matthew 2. Recruit a volunteer to read aloud Matthew 2:7-12. Ask:

- How does the story of the magi ("wise men") in Matthew connect to the theme of light we discussed in John's "Christmas story"?
- What does this story say about who holds true power and authority? How?
- Hamilton speculates the magi, who were Persian astrologers and priests, may have believed Jesus was the *Saoshyant*, or messiah, of the Zoroastrian religion. "I love," he writes, "what this story says about the wideness of God's mercy" (page 158). What do you think the story says about God's mercy? How should the example of the magi influence our relationship to people of other faiths today?

- Hamilton writes that though the magi's gifts to the young Jesus may have symbolic meaning, he thinks it likely Matthew's "primary reference" in mentioning them was to evoke a prophecy of Isaiah. Read Isaiah 60:1-7. What does God promise to the people in these verses? Why does Matthew connect this prophecy to Jesus?

- For Hamilton, the story of the magi kneeling before Jesus illustrates the New Testament's most commonly used title for Jesus and one of the most important: *Lord*. What does it mean for you to call Jesus *Lord*? How, specifically, do you "kneel before" him in your daily living? What treasures—tangible and otherwise—do you present to him for his use, as the magi opened their treasure chests?

Closing Your Session

Remind participants of the titles for Jesus which they have explored during this study (you may want to write them on the large sheets of paper or markerboard):

- Messiah (Anointed One)
- King
- Savior
- Emmanuel
- Word of God
- Light
- Lord

Ask:

- Which of these titles from the Christmas stories mean more to you as a result of our study of *Incarnation*? Which, if any, do you still find challenging, and why?
- How has our study of *Incarnation* changed your experience and observance of this Advent and Christmas season?

Express your gratitude for participants and for the study, and be sure to answer these questions yourself as part of the discussion.

Close your session and your study using a ritual modeled on Adam Hamilton's description of the Christmas candlelight service at the Church of the Resurrection:

- Distribute unlit candles or electric votives to participants. Again, darken your meeting space. Re-light or turn back on the large candle.
- Tell participants: "Jesus said, 'I am the light of the world,' but he also told his disciples, 'You, together, are the light of the world.'"
- Read aloud Matthew 5:14-16; then read aloud from *Incarnation*:

"In our world, you're either bringing darkness or light. By your words and deeds, you bring joy, love, and hope to others or you take it away. You bless and build up or you tear down and hurt. Life is either all about you or it is about others." (page 146)

- Light one participant's candle from the large candle and have participants light one another's candles (or have participants turn on their electric votives one at a time). Each person should say, "The light of Christ."
- Close with the prayer at the end of *Incarnation*, Chapter 4; the prayer below; or one of your own.

Dear Jesus, we acclaim you with many titles and names, but they all point us to your presence, power, and love. May we shine with your light not only at Christmas but at all times, in all our words and deeds. As you took on human flesh in a unique and decisive way so long ago, may you, in smaller but significant ways, take it on again in our flesh, that the world may see and give glory to your Father in heaven and ours. Amen.

Optional Extension

In Chapter 4, Hamilton mentions a prayer attributed to St. Francis of Assisi. Sing or read together "Make Me a Channel of Your Peace," a hymn setting this prayer to music (https://hymnary.org/text/make_me_a_channel_of_ your_peace). Ask participants to think of specific times they have received and/or given God's light in ways the lyrics describe.

Made in the USA
Coppell, TX
03 November 2020

40719017R00036